Can You Afford
to Grow Old?

By

Richard M. Nathanson
Principal, The Abby Group

Library of Congress Card Catalog Number: 98-91229

ISBN: 1-57502-735-6

Seventh Printing 2003

Printed in the USA by
Morris Publishing
3212 East Highway 30
Kearney, NE 68847
1-800-650-7888

Table of Contents

Prologue   1

Chapter 1
    The Aging of America   3

Chapter 2
    What Is Long Term Care?   5

Chapter 3
    The Need for Long Term Care   7

Chapter 4
    Why Buy Long Term Care Insurance?   11

Chapter 5
    The Medicare Program   15

Chapter 6
    The Medicaid Program   19

Chapter 7
    Buy Now or Wait?   25

Chapter 8
    Should You Self-Insure?   29

Table of Contents

Chapter 9
    Selecting the Right Policy   33

Chapter 10
    Tax-Qualified Plans vs. Non-Qualified Plans   67

Chapter 11
    Caveat Emptor...Let the Buyer Beware   73

Chapter 12
    Distribution Sources for Purchasing Long Term
    Care Insurance   79

Chapter 13
    Financial Strength of the Company   81

Chapter 14
    The Application Process   83

Chapter 15
    Underwriting   87

Chapter 16
    Epilogue   89

Table of Contents

Appendices

I. Glossary of Terms   91

II. Sample Underwriting Guideline   97

III. About the Author   101

Order Form   104

Free Consultation   106

Martha Mirman

I first met Martha Mirman on October 10, 1982. At the time, I was dating her granddaughter, soon to be my wife, and we decided to take a trip to Disneyworld. Martha, who was then 80 years old, came up from Bal Harbour, Florida, to join us in Orlando.

I hadn't met many people who were in their 80s. My grandparents had all passed away at much earlier ages, when I was in my teens. So I didn't know what to expect.

Surprisingly, Martha was a very energetic, alert individual who had interests that ranged from football to politics. She went to the theater every week, dined out three times per week, had the obligatory Saturday beauty parlor appointment, and still drove her car every day.

If Martha typified what it meant to grow old, it didn't seem so bad.

Unfortunately, like many people her age, Martha grew a little unsteady on her feet. One day Martha was bending over to pick up her mail, and she fell and broke her hip.

That was in 1990.

After her hip healed, Martha changed. She was no longer a spry senior citizen but, rather, someone who no longer felt that she could take care of herself.

Richard Nathanson

From 1990 to 1996 Martha needed care. She lived with my wife and me for a couple of years and spent the last four years in a group family home. I learned firsthand that the cost of care is not cheap.

For 6 years our family spent $3,000 per month providing care for Martha.

Martha passed away in 1996 at the age of 92.

The cost of Martha's care totaled $216,000. That is $216,000 less money that my mother-in-law has to live on.

A prospective client once said to me, "I am not going to buy long term care insurance because I feel insurance-poor." And he didn't buy it. Three years later, I ran into his wife and she told me he had suffered a stroke and has been in a nursing home for two years.

Being (insurance) poor may have applied then, but the meaning of poor changes completely when you pay out $3,000 per month for a nursing home.

This book is dedicated to Martha Mirman, for without the knowledge and experiences I have gained from dealing with the consequences of her growing old, I would not have written this book.

The Aging of America

The need for long term care is a relatively new phenomenon.

Part of the problem is due to the fact that the senior population is growing at an increasing rate. By the year 2030 the United States' population is projected to grow 22%, with seniors accounting for most of that growth. In fact, the 65-74 age bracket is projected to grow 104% and the over-85 age bracket is projected to grow 160%.

This population growth is due in large part to increasing life expectancies. At the turn of this century life expectancies were in the early 50s; now, if you reach age 75, your life expectancy is age 85.

And this trend is expected to continue into the next century.

Medical advances are having a dramatic impact on lengthening our lives. One reason that cognitive-impairment problems like Alzheimer's disease are such a problem today is that in the past, people passed away before Alzheimer's manifested itself. Former President Reagan's Alzheimer's attests to the fact that you can live a long time with a degenerative disease.

Before recent medical advances, most people passed away from acute medical problems like heart attacks and strokes. Now the majority of elderly people are faced with more chronic situations that are more easily controled by advancing medical procedures and medicines.

Richard Nathanson

Social changes have also had an impact on the senior population.

I lived for 42 years in Boston, Massachusetts, and moved to Seattle, Washington. My mother still lives in Boston. If my mother needs care, there is not the kind of family support system available that was prevalent in families 20 or 30 years ago. More families have two working parents. The lack of job security, a problem of the '90s, forces working individuals to be more mobile in their job selection. Unfortunately, it is now more and more difficult to rely on a family member to provide care for an elderly parent.

Regrettably, the aging of America is a double-edged sword. We all enjoy the prospects of a longer healthy life, but, when the biological clock causes chronic medical conditions or, as in the case of Martha Mirman, a broken hip requires 6 years of care, there is no way to minimize the problem of needing long term care.

Chapter 2

What Is Long Term Care?

You are receiving long term care when you need day-in-and-day-out assistance because you have either a serious medical problem or a functional disability that lasts for a period time, resulting in your inability to care for yourself.

Most people erroneously think of long term care as solely a result of a medical problem. In reality, people with acute medical problems either get better or pass away. With an acute medical problem, your life expectancy is not great.

In contrast, it is the functional disability that precipitates most long term care needs. The person who had a stroke and can no longer feed or dress himself needs long term care. The elderly woman who is so unsteady that she needs help to walk needs long term care. The individual who can no longer bathe or take care of basic personal hygiene needs long term care. The person who must wear an adult diaper because of an incontinence problem needs long term care.

There are three different levels of care that you can receive in a long term care environment.

Skilled care is defined as the kind of care you would receive in a hospital setting by skilled nursing practitioners. It is primarily for seriously ill people who need continuous medical attention. Generally speaking, the person is bedridden and under 24-hour medical supervision. Statistics show that only 0.5% of people receiving care require skilled nursing care.

The second level of care is *intermediate care*, which is typically care that requires occasional services like physical therapy or intermittent medical care such as help with administering medications. This level of care accounts for only 4.5% of all care received in a long term setting.

The most important level of care is *custodial care*. Custodial care is the kind of care that most people would receive in a nursing home, assisted living facility, or home care setting. Custodial care represents the majority of care (95%) that people receive in a long term care setting.

Custodial care provides assistance with activities that we take for granted. These activities are known as activities of daily living (ADLs). The ADLs consist of such basic functions as mobility, dressing, bathing, toileting, maintaining continence, transferring, and eating.

The degree to which you need help with these activities varies with the degree of your functional disability.

The least impaired person would first need help with mobility, as this is the first ADL that most people have difficulty with. If you have ever been in a nursing home, you probably noted that almost everyone is using a walker, cane, or wheelchair.

After mobility, dressing and bathing are generally the next level of impairment. It would be at this level of impairment that you would pass the threshold of eligibility with almost all long term care policies.

The most severely impaired individuals would need help with the remaining ADLs. This level of impairment might necessitate a nursing home or assisted living arrangement.

Chapter 3

The Need for Long Term Care

When I conduct seminars on long term care, I always ask a couple of questions.

"Who in this room knows someone who has needed long term care"?

Virtually everyone raises a hand.

Then I ask, "Who in this room thinks that <u>you</u> will need long term care?"

No one ever raises a hand.

That is the problem with long term care. Everyone knows the problem exists, but everyone thinks it will happen to someone else.

Statistics and probabilities only tell part of the problem. Odds and probabilities of needing long term care are interesting, but **when it happens to you, the odds become 100%.**

You are not unusual if you are worried about needing care in your old age.

The facts prove that your worries are real:

Fact... 43% of people over age 65 will spend time in a nursing home.

Fact... 7 out of 10 couples will have at least one partner using nursing home care.

Fact... 15% of women will spend more than 5 years in a nursing home.

Fact... 4% of men will spend more than 5 years in a nursing home.

Fact... Average nursing home stay is 2.5 years, which does not include time spent receiving care at home or care at an assisted living facility.

Fact... Today's cost of an average nursing home stay is $100,000.

Fact... In 20 years at 5% inflation, an average nursing home stay will cost $265,000.

Fact... Nursing home populations are 71% female.

Fact... Of those who enter a nursing home for the long haul, half will become destitute within 6 months.

Fact... Fewer than one-tenth of elderly nursing home patients can afford to pay for a year of nursing home care solely out of their income.

The facts are not on our side, and the aging of America will only continue to exacerbate the long term care problem.

Some people will always be in denial. "The problem will not affect me but someone else." "I am healthy and I will never need care."

Some of my clients even say they will call Dr. Kevorkian rather than go to a nursing home. I jokingly respond that if you have Alzheimer's disease, you probably will have forgotten Dr. Kevorkian's phone number.

Can You Afford to Grow Old?

Don't wait until it is too late. People do need care and the care is expensive.

If Martha Mirman had had long term care insurance, my mother-in-law would have $216,000 more than she has today.

Richard Nathanson

Chapter 4

Why Buy Long Term Care Insurance?

The reasons for buying long term care insurance generally fall into two broad areas.

Reason #1... If you need long term care, the cost of the care can be financially devastating. An extended need can wipe out what a person has worked their lifetime to accumulate. As I mentioned earlier, in my family, we spent $216,000 paying for the care of Martha Mirman. It is for that very reason, the protection of assets, that people purchase long term care insurance.

Assume for a moment that average nursing home costs are $130 per day. With an average nursing home stay of 2.5 years, the financial risk is $118,625. Add 1.5 years of home care, which can also run $130 per day, then the financial risk increases to $189,800. A married couple is subject to double the risk.

The question must be asked, "Can I afford $189,800 ($379,600 for married couples) for the cost of needing care?"

Additionally, the younger you are, the greater the financial risk. The reason... inflation. If nursing home care rises at the rate of 5% per year, then your financial risk rises significantly over time.

The chart on the next page reflects that increasing risk.

Potential Out-of-Pocket Costs per Person

Risk Today	$189,800
Risk 5 Years From Now	$242,944
Risk 10 Years From Now	$309,374
Risk 15 Years From Now	$394,784

If you are now age 55, by the time you are age 70, inflation has increased the financial risk per person to $394,784.

Exacerbating the potential out-of-pocket expenses is the fact that with the improvements in medical science and likely longer life expectancies, the risk of inflation dramatically increases the overall financial exposure.

One must ask the question, "Can I afford this risk?"

The only person who ultimately gambles on long term care insurance is the one who goes without it.

The risk of needing care is always there; it is just the question of who holds the risk...your family or the long term care insurance company?

Reason #2...The second reason for purchasing long term care insurance is for peace of mind.

Can You Afford to Grow Old?

Peace of mind is viewed in many different ways. The knowledge that you can remain financially independent gives peace of mind. The ability to maintain personal control over your life gives you peace of mind. The ability to avoid being dependent on someone else gives you peace of mind.

I like to look at peace of mind a little differently.

Think about someone you know who is receiving care. In reality, a family member is usually involved in making the arrangements and decisions. Hopefully the family member doesn't also have to take financial responsibility.

I view that long term care insurance is not really for the peace of mind of the insured but, rather, for the peace of mind of the family member who will ultimately take responsibility for the person needing care.

There is an old adage in the life insurance business: you won't buy life insurance unless you love someone. You also have to love someone to buy the peace of mind that long term care insurance offers.

Richard Nathanson

Chapter 5

The Medicare Program

Medicare is a national health insurance program that is available primarily to individuals 65 years of age and older. Medicare consists of two parts.

Part A helps pay for care in a hospital, care in a skilled nursing facility, and hospice care. During the first 60 days, Medicare pays all covered hospital costs except for the first $764. That is the hospital deductible for 1998. For days 61 through 90 in a benefit period, Medicare pays all covered hospital costs except for coinsurance ($191 per day in 1998).

Part B helps pay for doctor bills and for outpatient hospital care and other medical services not covered by Part A. Typically such services consist of X rays and laboratory tests, certain ambulance services, and durable medical equipment. In addition Part B pays for physical and occupational therapy, speech and language therapy, and pathology services.

Contrary to public opinion, Medicare typically pays very little for long term care needs. In fact, despite a persistent myth, hardly any long term care costs--about 2%--are covered by Medicare and Medigap policies.

Medicare will pay for a limited stay in a nursing home under very specified and restrictive conditions.

When Does Medicare Pay for Nursing Home Care?

The following conditions must be met for Medicare to pay for nursing home care.

Richard Nathanson

The patient must be admitted to a hospital for at least 3 consecutive days prior to being sent to a Medicare-approved skilled nursing facility. The day of discharge from the hospital does not count as one of the 3 days. The patient's physician must certify that the patient needs skilled nursing or rehabilitation services on a daily basis, and the care must be restorative in nature.

The patient must be admitted to the skilled nursing facility for the same condition that resulted in hospital treatment. The patient must be admitted to the skilled nursing facility within 30 days of discharge from the hospital.

Real-Life Story... *I first met Mr. & Mrs. Bend a couple of years ago when Mr. Bend was suffering from Alzheimer's disease. Mrs. Bend was providing daily care, but eventually his care needs surpassed her abilities to care for him. She decided she had to send her husband to a nursing home. The problem... the physician could not admit Mr. Bend to the hospital because he didn't have an acute medical problem.*

Medicare paid nothing.

Real-Life Story... *Mrs. Wilson, who lived in Bellevue, Washington, was out one day walking her dog and she tripped on the curb and fell. Medical diagnosis... broken hip. She was sent to the hospital, satisfied the 3-day prior hospital stay requirement and was sent to a skilled nursing facility for rehabilitation. So far no problem and Medicare paid.*

Just prior to her discharge from the nursing home, she suffered a minor stroke. Because skilled nursing care was now required for a condition that did not send her to the hospital, she was not in compliance with the Medicare rules.

Medicare paid nothing.

Can You Afford to Grow Old?

Real-Life Story... *Mr. Smith was a client I met a number of years ago. He was diagnosed 5 years before with Parkinson's disease. Unfortunately, Parkinson's disease is a degenerative neurological affliction that could eventually require nursing home care. Over the years Mr. Smith's condition deteriorated to the point where his wife felt that he needed to be admitted to a nursing home. She was also aware of the 3-day prior hospital stay. Her husband's physician admitted Mr. Smith to the hospital and he stayed there the requisite 3 days. He was then discharged to the skilled nursing facility. His disease progressed to the point where the only care that was needed was personal or custodial care. He needed help with daily activities like bathing, dressing, walking, etc. However, Medicare does not pay unless your care is restorative in nature.*

Medicare paid nothing.

Unfortunately, these situations are not unique. Keep in mind that Medicare is primarily a medical insurance program. Thus, Medicare is not a substitute for long term care insurance.

If you are lucky enough to satisfy and comply with all of the Medicare rules, Medicare will pay 100% of approved charges for the first 20 days of care in a skilled nursing facility. For the next 80 days, Medicare will pay all approved charges less the 1997 daily co-payment of $95.00-per-day. Individuals with either a Medigap policy or who belong to an HMO plan generally do not have to pay the $95.00-per-day co-pay.

After 100 days Medicare pays nothing.

Richard Nathanson

The reality is that Medicare is not the solution to the long term care problem.

"The public mistakenly believes that Medicare--the nation's health insurance program for those over 65--is supposed to pay for their long term care."   --Los Angeles Times, *May 5, 1995*

Chapter 6

The Medicaid Program

Medicaid is a state and federally funded medical assistance program for certain people, including the elderly and disabled, that will pay 100% of nursing home costs.

Medicaid is essentially a welfare program. To be eligible you must satisfy strict asset and income limitations.

In the state of Washington, the Department of Social and Health Services (DSHS) administers the Medicaid program.

Medicaid is often the least desirable option available for long term institutional care.

Medicaid Eligibility Requirements

The complexity of the Medicaid program requires consultation with an attorney who specializes in Medicaid. There are two tests that must be met: an asset test and an income test.

Asset Test

Nonexempt resources for an individual must not exceed $2,000. All assets are included for purposes of the asset test unless specifically determined to be exempt. See below for exempt resources.

Spouses may not have combined nonexempt resources in excess of $79,020 (as of January 1997). Assets of both spouses are considered in determining this amount.

The spouse at home may be allowed more than $79,020 of nonexempt resources if the total income of both spouses is not enough to provide the spouse at home with income equal to the basic spousal income maintenance allowance. To get this, the spouse at home must obtain the consent of DSHS that more resources are necessary to produce the needed income.

Exempt Resources

Exempt resources are not counted as a part of the $79,020 and $2,000 resource limits. Some of these resources are:

• The home is exempt if the Medicaid recipient or spouse, or dependent relative, lives in the home. The proceeds from the sale of the home are exempt if another home is purchased within 3 months of the date when the proceeds become available. If no spouse or qualified dependent relative lives in the home, the home may be exempt if the applicant intends to return to the home.

• Furnishings, clothing, and ordinary household and personal items that provide the essentials of living, basic comfort, and convenience are exempt.

• One automobile is exempt. In the case of one spouse in a nursing home, the second spouse's car is exempt regardless of value. In the case of a single person, the car is exempt if its value does not exceed $4,500, unless a more expensive car is needed for special circumstances.

• A life insurance policy is exempt if the face value does not exceed $1,500. If the face value of the policy exceeds $1,500, the entire amount of the cash surrender value of the policy is counted as a resource.

Can You Afford to Grow Old?

- Prepaid burial contracts and funds set aside for burial of the Medicaid applicant and spouse are exempt if the amounts set aside do not exceed $1,500 for each spouse. Burial spaces for the Medicaid applicant and the immediate family are exempt regardless of value.

- Pension funds owned by the non-Medicaid applicant spouse are not counted. Pension funds owned by the Medicaid applicant are counted.

- Sales contracts may or may not be counted, depending on other available resources, when the sales contract was entered into, the terms of the contract, or whether it was from the sale of the primary residence.

Income Test

As with the case of the asset test, the income rules are complex and often confusing. Consultation with an attorney is recommended.

- The Medicaid applicant's income must be less than the institution's Medicaid rate plus regular monthly medical expenses. The Medicaid rate for nursing homes varies and changes periodically.

Deductions

The Medicaid recipient is allowed certain deductions from income received. Examples of the deductions are:

- A monthly personal needs allowance of $41.62.

- A monthly spousal maintenance allowance.

- An allowance for dependent family members living with the spouse at home.

- Health insurance and Medicare premiums.

- Court-ordered guardianship fees when approved by the state.

Rules Pertaining to Gifting Assets

There is no prohibition of or penalty for selling assets for fair value. However, if assets are gifted away, the Medicaid applicant may be ineligible for Medicaid for a period of time. There is no longer a maximum period of ineligibility.

Gifts to Non-Spouses

Gifts made within 36 months of applying for Medicaid eligibility are taken into account and may result in periods of Medicaid ineligibility.

Gifts of Exempt Resources

Generally, the transfer of exempt resources does not result in a period of Medicaid ineligibility.

A home may be transferred without resulting in a period of Medicaid ineligibility if transferred to:

- A spouse

- A child who has lived in the home and cared for the Medicaid applicant/parent for 2 years before the parent enters the nursing home, or a child who is under the age of 21, blind, or totally and permanently disabled

Can You Afford to Grow Old?

- A brother or sister who has an equity interest in the home and has lived in the home for 1 year immediately before the Medicaid applicant entered the nursing home

Gifts to Trusts

New rules apply to trusts created after August 10, 1993. The look-back period has been increased to 60 months. In addition, in most cases in which the applicant can receive either principal or income from the trust, the assets of the trust or the income will be deemed to be an available resource.

Ineligibility Period

All gifts of assets made within 36 months of Medicaid application are taken into consideration. This is called the "look-back period." As stated above, this look-back period is 60 months in the case of transfers to trusts. There is no maximum period of ineligibility. The exact period of ineligibility is determined by dividing the average nursing home cost in the state of Washington ($4,013 as of October 1, 1997) into the total value of all gifts made within the look-back period. For example, if the gift of assets totaled $401,300 then the ineligibility period would be 100 months ($401,300/$4,013 =100 months).

The period of ineligibility begins on the first day of the month within the look-back period in which an asset was transferred.

Recommendation... *Generally speaking, if Medicaid is a viable option it means that your assets and income approach the asset and income limitation. In such circumstances it probably would not be necessary to purchase long term care insurance.*

Richard Nathanson

Chapter 7

Buy Now or Wait?

For most people, the timing of when to purchase a long term care policy is often quite difficult. Most people think they are healthy. They expect to be healthy. So why spend the money now on a premium when the expectation of needing care is not for quite a while?

I don't recommend purchasing a policy if you are less than 50 years old, unless you have a unique medical situation. The ages of 50 to 70 are usually the best time to buy a policy. Most people are still healthy and the premiums are reasonably affordable. For those over age 70, premiums take a big increase and health problems make it more difficult to get approved for coverage.

There are two problems with waiting.

The first is health. You have to be relatively healthy to purchase a long term care policy. Health can and does change and usually for the worst. There are many health situations that will either temporarily delay your ability to purchase the insurance or permanently eliminate your ability to purchase the coverage. Refer to appendix II for a typical underwriting guide.

Real-Life Story... *Mr. and Mrs. Allen decided to purchase long term care insurance. They were in their early 60s and appeared to be in good health. I was in the process of completing the application for Mr. and Mrs. Allen, when Mr. Allen told me that his doctor was considering a minor hernia repair. The result... Mr. Allen was uninsurable until after the surgery.*

Anticipated surgery is just one of many health situations that can delay the ability to get insured.

Real-Life Story... *I was in the process of putting together a plan for Mr. Badenberg. After a series of meetings, he just wasn't sure how concerned he was about long term care. He also didn't know whether he wanted to invest $2,000 per year for a plan. Mr. Badenberg subsequently was diagnosed with rheumatoid arthritis. Now he is uninsurable. He now recognizes the need for long term care and suddenly the $2,000-per-year premium is a small cost relative to the risk. Unfortunately, nothing can be done right now... Mr. Badenberg waited too long.*

The second problem with waiting is cost. Long term care policies cost more the older you are. The longer you wait, the significantly more expensive it can become.

The following chart illustrates the financial consequences of waiting.

The Cost of Waiting

Age	Buy at Age 69	Buy at Age 75
69	$2,110	$0
70	$2,110	$0
71	$2,110	$0
72	$2,110	$0
73	$2,110	$0
74	$2,110	$0
75	$2,110	$5,694
76	$2,110	$5,694
77	$2,110	$5,694
78	$2,110	$5,694
79	$2,110	$5,694
80	$2,110	$5,694
Total Premiums	$25,320	$34,164

Can You Afford to Grow Old?

The chart shows the actual cost of a plan, assuming the person purchased it at age 69 and paid the premiums through age 80 and needed care at age 81. This person would have paid a total of $25,320 in premiums.

The person who waited bought the plan at age 75, paid the premium through age 80, and needed care at age 81. This person would have paid a total of $34,164 in premiums.

Besides more out-of-pocket outlay, the person who waited had to hope that during the period from age 69 to 74 his health remained constant and that he could even buy the policy at age 75.

Recommendation... *If you are over age 50, seriously evaluate the problem of long term care. If you think it fits into your overall planning requirements, buy the policy sooner rather than later.*

Richard Nathanson

Chapter 8

Should You Self-Insure?

Frequently, people who are considering long term care insurance make the following statements.

"I am young and in good health. Doesn't it make sense for me to take the premium that I would spend on long term care insurance and invest that money to provide for my long term care?"

No, it doesn't make sense.

Let's make a couple of assumptions.

- You are age 55.

- You buy a policy that will pay $130 per day.

- You buy a policy that will pay for 4 years.

- You buy a policy that has 5% compound inflation.

- The actual premium would be $1,274 per year.

OR

- You could invest the premium and get a return of 10% per year.

How much money could you accumulate in 25 years to pay for your care, as compared to how much money the policy would pay out for your care?

Investing the Premium Equivalent of $1,274 per year at 10%

Year	Value at end of year
Year 1	$ 1,401
Year 2	$ 2,943
Year 3	$ 4,638
Year 4	$ 6,504
Year 5	$ 8,556
Year 6	$ 10,813
Year 7	$ 13,295
Year 8	$ 16,026
Year 9	$ 19,030
Year 10	$ 22,335
Year 11	$ 25,970
Year 12	$ 29,967
Year 13	$ 34,366
Year 14	$ 39,204
Year 15	$ 44,526
Year 16	$ 50,380
Year 17	$ 56,819
Year 18	$ 63,903
Year 19	$ 71,694
Year 20	$ 80,265
Year 21	$ 89,693
Year 22	$100,063
Year 23	$111,472
Year 24	$124,020
Year 25	$137,824

At age 80 you would have $137,824 available for your care.

Can You Afford to Grow Old?

Growth of the Maximum Benefit of the LTC Policy

Year	Value at end of year
Year 1	$199,290
Year 2	$209,254
Year 3	$219,717
Year 4	$230,703
Year 5	$242,238
Year 6	$254,350
Year 7	$267,067
Year 8	$280,421
Year 9	$294,442
Year 10	$309,164
Year 11	$324,622
Year 12	$340,853
Year 13	$357,896
Year 14	$375,791
Year 15	$394,580
Year 16	$414,309
Year 17	$435,025
Year 18	$456,776
Year 19	$479,615
Year 20	$503,595
Year 21	$528,775
Year 22	$555,214
Year 23	$582,975
Year 24	$612,124
Year 25	$642,730

At age 80 you would have $642,730 available for your care.

The bottom line... If you decided to self-insure and invest the amount of money that you would have paid for a long term care premium, you would have accumulated $137,824 for your care.

If you invested in a long term care policy, you would have had $642,730 available for your care.

Thus, by purchasing the long term care policy you would have 466% more money available to you than if you had self-insured.

The self-insuring option also presupposes that you have a long time to invest the premium dollars.

What would happen if you had only 10 years and at age 65 you suffered a stroke and needed care?

With the self-insuring option you would have accumulated $22,335 that could be spent on your care.

With a long term care policy, the maximum benefit would be $309,164 that could be spent on your care.

The long term care policy would have 1,380% more money available to you than if you had self-insured.

Recommendation... *If you are concerned about the problem of long term care and the potential catastrophic out-of-pocket expenses, it is more prudent to purchase the insurance than to self-insure.*

Chapter 9

Selecting the Right Policy

When I help my clients select the right long term care plan, the process boils down to two aspects: cost and features. These two items are inexorably linked and you need to look at the interaction of the two items. If the least expensive policy doesn't contain the features that you want, the policy doesn't make any sense. Similarly, if the policy with the best features is out of your price range, it too doesn't make sense.

The first step in the process is to look at cost estimates from a number of companies. It's human nature that consumers are immediately drawn to the least expensive plan. You also need to look at the features of the particular policy. If the least expensive policy contains the best features, then it is an easy match. If the policy with the best features is not the least expensive, then you must evaluate and ask the question, "Am I prepared to spend extra money per month to get the features that I want?"

Cost Factors

There are six elements in determining the cost of a long term care policy.

• Age

This is a variable we can not control.

Unlike with a life insurance policy, with a long term care policy your "insurance age" is your "actual age" at the time you sign the application. Generally, the older you are, the more expensive the plan is. Once you purchase a policy, however, the premiums are designed not to go up as you get older. (See Chapter 11, Caveat Emptor... Let the Buyer Beware.)

• Health

You need to be healthy to purchase long term care insurance. The insurance company, however, determines health, and there is a great deal of variation in underwriting between companies.

Some companies will either approve you or deny you at the stated premium. Other companies have higher rates if your health does not warrant the lowest rate. If you are in less than perfect health, ask the agent what underwriting class he thinks you will be accepted at.

• Daily Benefit Amount

This is the amount that the company will pay on a daily basis for your care. Available options range from $40 per day to $200 per day. At the present time, nursing home care is averaging $130 per day to $150 per day. Home care is averaging $15 per hour. In choosing the daily benefit amount, you must take into consideration how much of the risk you want to transfer to the insurance company. Most of my clients have selected between $100 and $150 per day. The clients who select the lower range feel that it is appropriate to self-insure a portion of the risk. The clients who select the higher range want to have almost all of the risk transferred to the insurance company.

• Duration

This is how long the policy will pay for. Available options range from a low of 1 year to as long as lifetime. Bear in mind the duration does not start until you first need care. For example, if you purchased a 4-year policy at age 65 and didn't need care until age 75, the 4 years would commence at age 75.

The duration is by far the hardest number to select in putting together a plan. You can be guided by average statistics. But if you pick a 4-year plan and you need care the 5th year, that year of unreimbursed care will cost you a lot of money.

If it's affordable, pick a duration of lifetime, which means the policy will pay for as long as you need care. If that's not possible, select a plan with a duration of between 3 and 5 years, which tends to cover the average need.

- **Elimination Period**

This is the number of days that you must pay before the policy pays. Available options range from a low of 0 days (policy pays on first day of eligibility) to as long as 365 days. The most common elimination period is 100 days. As discussed in the Medicare section, up to 100 days may be paid by Medicare.

If you select the 100-day option, purchase the plan based on the assumption that you will have to pay the first 100 days out of your pocket. If Medicare pays any of those days, consider it an early birthday present.

- **Inflation Factor**

The various inflation options are discussed later in this chapter. Inflation protection provides that your daily benefit amount will increase by a predetermined amount on an annual basis. Inflation protection is designed to help assure that the daily benefit amount keeps pace with rising nursing home or home health care costs.

These six variables will determine the cost of the premium.

Do rates vary between companies?

The answer is yes, and the numbers may be quite surprising.

The rates below are actual premiums for one person at the company's lowest/best rate based on health. It includes a daily benefit amount of $100 per day, a 4-year duration, compound inflation, and a 100-day elimination period (policy C has a 90-day elimination period).

Actual Rate Comparison
(rate in boldface is the lowest rate)

Age	Policy A	Policy B	Policy C
50	$ 980	$ 840	**$ 779**
55	$ 980	$ 940	**$ 894**
60	**$1,110**	$1,250	$1,181
64	**$1,110**	$1,600	$1,525
69	**$1,800**	$2,250	$2,197
70	$2,490	$2,440	**$2,386**
71	$2,680	$2,660	**$2,599**
72	$2,860	$2,900	**$2,837**
73	$3,160	$3,170	**$3,116**
74	$3,450	$3,460	**$3,411**
75	**$3,720**	$3,777	$3,756
76	**$3,980**	$4,100	$4,100
77	**$4,230**	$4,460	$4,494
78	**$4,710**	$4,820	$4,920
79	**$5,180**	$5,200	$5,354
80	$5,640	**$5,610**	N/A

Can You Afford to Grow Old?

A couple of observations should be made.

The greatest variations in premiums occur between ages 60 and 69. Within that age bracket, at age 64 the difference between the highest and the lowest premium is a whooping 44%.

Between ages 50 and 59, the average difference in premium is around 17%.

Between ages 70 and 80, there is statistically very little difference in premiums, with the difference generally no greater than 3%.

On the basis of cost alone, it pays to review many different plans. When you couple the differences in cost with the differences in the features among the plans, it is essential to review many different plans.

Analysis of Various Features

Now that we have explored the factors affecting cost and illustrated the potential significant differences in cost, the next and probably more difficult part of the process is to analyze the difference in how the policy works.

This section discusses in detail some of the key elements to look for in a long term care policy. Following the discussion of each feature, I make a recommendation as to the importance of the particular feature.

Review the features, the discussions, and the Real-Life Stories, and try to evaluate which features are important to you.

I am frequently asked, "Does one policy contain every single best feature on the market today"?

Unfortunately, the answer is no. If one policy had the best features for everyone, the selection process would be pretty easy. To help facilitate the process, however, after the recommendation section, I have included a rating category. The ratings range from 1 to 10. A rating of 1 indicates that the scope of the feature is very important, whereas a higher numerical rating indicates a feature has potentially less value when you are selecting a particular policy.

Do You Purchase a Comprehensive Plan or a Stand Alone Plan?

This is the first step in selecting a long term care policy.

You must decide whether you want a policy that will pay for your care wherever you want it, i.e., nursing home, assisted living, adult day care, hospice care, and/or home care.

Or do you want a policy that will cover you in only one or two of those settings?

Most people select the comprehensive plan. Obviously, nobody knows where he or she will need to receive care, and most people want to have complete flexibility. However, there can be situations in which a limited plan is appropriate.

Real-Life Story... *Mr. Paul, one of my existing clients, lives alone. His wife recently suffered a stroke and was confined to a nursing home. Mr. Paul is "old- fashioned." His wife did virtually everything for him. With his wife's absence, cooking is now a chore. At the point when Mr. Jones needs care, he would be unable to stay totally independent at home. He would want to move to an assisted living facility where he can still have his own independent space, with meals and care also available. Mr. Paul*

Can You Afford to Grow Old?

purchased a nursing home and assisted living facility policy only. It was the right policy for him.

Recommendation... *If total flexibility is important, purchase only a comprehensive policy.*

Rating... 2

How Are the Dollar Benefits Calculated?

All polices pay up to the daily benefit amount for a certain duration. The duration can be calculated based on either a "pool of money" basis or a "number of days" basis.

A "pool of money" works this way. Let's assume you purchase $100-per-day daily benefit and want the plan to last 4 years. There are 1,460 days in 4 years. Under "the pool of money" concept, the $100 per day is multiplied by the 1,460 days, which creates a maximum benefit of $146,000.

Under this method, your benefit will last as long as the maximum benefit of $146,000 lasts. If you spend the money at the rate of $100 per day then it will last 4 years. If you spend less than $100 per day, the money will last longer.

Under the "number of days" method, if you purchase $100 per day for 4 years, the benefit will last only 4 years. If you spend less than the $100 per day the unused money is lost.

Recommendation... *If you purchase a realistic amount of daily benefit, then there is no difference between the "pool of money" concept and the "number of days" method. Additionally, if you purchase a lifetime benefit, meaning the company will pay the daily benefit amount for as long as you need care, then there is no difference in the methods. Only if you spend less per day than* *the daily benefit amount can the "pool of money" method be advantageous.*

Rating... 4

Are the Benefit Amounts Combined or Separate?

If your policy allows you to receive your care in a nursing home or community-based/home care, then there are two possible ways of calculating how much care you can receive in each setting.

The first are separate benefit amounts. For example, your policy may provide for 2 years of nursing home care and 2 years of home care.

<table>
<tr><td>2 Years
Nursing Home
Care</td><td>2 Years
Home Care</td></tr>
</table>

Under this scenario, view the straight line above as a barrier. If you received 2 years in home care and want to continue receiving care in your home, your policy will not pay and you are out of luck.

If you received 2 years of nursing home care and you need to stay in the nursing home longer, your policy will not pay and you are out of luck.

Can You Afford to Grow Old?

Other policies will combine your benefit amounts.

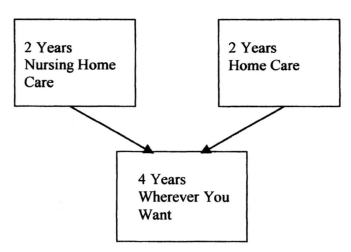

In this case you can receive the 4 years of care anyplace you want.

Real-Life Story... *I met Mr. Jones a number of years ago. Mr. Jones had a policy that had separate benefit amounts. He purchased 2 years of nursing home care and 2 years of home care. Mr. Jones suffered a massive stroke that required an immediate confinement to a nursing home. His 2 years in the nursing home were quickly extinguished. Mr. Jones was never able to go home again. He never used the 2 years of available home care. Mr. Jones passed away in the nursing home after 3.5 years. The last year and a half were paid for out of personal resources. If Mr. Jones had had an integrated policy, the insurance company would have paid for the entire duration of his nursing home confinement.*

Recommendation... *Always buy a policy that has an integrated benefit unless you purchase unlimited nursing home care and unlimited home care. In that case, even with separate benefit* *amounts, you would have an unlimited amount of coverage in the setting that you want.*

Rating...1

Is There a Distinction as to How Much a Policy Will Pay Out Depending upon the Location?

Unfortunately, yes.

You meet with a sales representative. You discuss benefit levels and determine that you want benefits of $100 per day. You think everything is all set.

Don't be so sure. Read your contract.

All policies will pay 100% of the daily benefit amount that you selected for care in a nursing home. However, many polices will tie the amount paid for an assisted living facility or home care to a certain percentage of the nursing home benefit. In general, if a policy is going to limit the amount paid in alternative settings, it will range from 50% to 80% of the daily benefit amount.

Real-Life Story... *I was once reviewing a policy for an individual and on the policy schedule page (the page that summarizes the benefits) it listed $150 per day for nursing home care and $150 per day for home care. However, the home care rider, which was on page 18 in a 20-page policy, indicated that if the person required custodial home care, then the policy would pay at 50% or $75 per day. The client was shocked. He thought he bought $150 per day. He wanted $150 per day. He didn't want $75 per day for home care.*

Can You Afford to Grow Old?

Recommendation... *If you select a certain dollar amount, make sure it pays that amount regardless of where you receive your care.*

Rating... 2

When Will a Long Term Care Policy Pay the Benefits?

This is the most important consideration in choosing a long term care policy. If your policy will not pay out the benefits that you expect, all other considerations become meaningless.

ADL Benefit Trigger

The first method of determining eligibility for payment is your inability to perform the Activities of Daily Living, commonly referred to as ADLs.

The following are common ADLs, along with their definitions.

Bathing...Washing oneself in either a tub or shower or sponge bath, including the task of getting into and out of the tub or shower without hands-on assistance of another person.

Dressing... Putting on and taking off all necessary and appropriate items of clothing and/or any necessary braces or artificial limbs without hands-on assistance of another person.

Toileting... Getting to and from the toilet, getting on and off the toilet, and performing associated personal hygiene without hands-on assistance of another person.

Transferring... Moving in and out of a bed, chair, or wheelchair without hands-on assistance of another person.

Eating...Getting nourishment into the body without hands-on assistance of another person once it has been prepared and made available to you.

Continence...Voluntarily maintaining control of bowel and/or bladder function in the event of incontinence and the ability to maintain a reasonable level of personal hygiene without hands-on assistance of another person.

In reviewing the definitions, read them closely. Note that eating does not include cooking the meals. Note that dressing and toileting do not include doing the laundry. Therefore, the policy will not pay for these activities unless a separate homemaker services benefit is available. This is discussed in more detail later in this chapter.

Presently all policies issued in the state of Washington base your eligibility for benefits on the inability to do a certain number of the ADLs. The number of the activities that you must be unable to perform varies among policies. Also the total number of eligible ADLs varies among companies.

The most common number is your inability to perform 3 out of 6 ADLs. The most liberal eligibility is the inability to perform just 1 ADL, and the greatest number of total ADLs is 7.

Companies that include the 7th ADL generally include mobility. Mobility, in addition to bathing, is generally the first activity that people start needing help with. It is critical that mobility and bathing are included in the list of ADLs.

Recommendation... *Select a policy that requires the inability to perform no more than 3 ADLs to determine eligibility. Make sure that the list of ADLs includes bathing and mobility.*

Rating...1

Can You Afford to Grow Old?

Cognitive Impairment Benefit Trigger

The second method of determining eligibility for benefits is whether you have a cognitive impairment problem. This is also referred to as senility or dementia; Alzheimer's disease falls into this category. All policies now issued in the state of Washington include a cognitive impairment trigger.

Medical Necessity Benefit Trigger

The third method of determining eligibility is whether you have a medical necessity. Not all policies offer this third way to qualify for benefits.

Real-Life Story... *Six years ago my aunt was diagnosed with ovarian cancer. Although she fought a battle that lasted 4 years, she eventually succumbed to her illness. Near the end of her life, she clearly had a medical problem. But despite the medical problem, she was able to perform all the ADLs. And despite the medical problem, she did not have a cognitive impairment problem. Therefore, if she had a policy that did not include the medical necessity trigger, she would not have been eligible for her benefits.*

Certain non-tax-qualified plans and all tax-qualified plans (discussed in detail later) do not include a medical necessity trigger.

Recommendation... *Do not buy a policy without all three ways to qualify. It makes no sense to limit, in any fashion, the possibility of qualifying for your benefits. In many ways it would be like buying a homeowners policy that covered damage from fire and theft only and not a policy that covered damage from fire, theft and windstorm.*

Rating...1

Richard Nathanson

Who Determines Your Eligibility?

There are two possible ways. The most common way is that your own physician certifies that you are unable to perform the ADLs, have a cognitive impairment problem, or have a medical problem.

However, certain policies require that the insurance company's doctor determine your eligibility.

Real-Life Story... *I met Mr. and Mrs. Evans last year. Mrs. Evans was starting to become concerned over her husband's short-term memory and suspected early Alzheimer's. Mrs. Evans' concern was based upon 30 years of living together and although the changes were subtle, she was aware of them. She filed a claim with her long term care company. Her policy required that the company's doctor determine a cognitive impairment problem. The insurance company's doctor performed standardized tests and the results were inconclusive. The company's doctor could not detect a cognitive impairment problem, although Mrs. Evans knew there was a problem. Claim denied.*

Recommendation...*You need every possible advocate on your side when you file a claim. Purchase a policy that allows your own doctor, who certainly will be an advocate for you, to determine your eligibility.*

Rating...1

What Inflation Options Are Available?

An inflation option provides that your daily benefit amount can periodically increase. There are four inflation options.

• The first is no inflation protection. This means that your daily benefit amount will never increase.

Can You Afford to Grow Old?

- The second method is an indexed method. This method generally provides you the opportunity of buying more coverage at predetermined intervals. If you elect the option to purchase more coverage, then you will pay an incremental increase in the premium based on how much more coverage you purchase and your current age.

- The third method is 5% simple inflation. With this method your daily benefit will increase a fixed 5% of the starting daily benefit amount. The premium will remain level.

- The fourth method is 5% compound inflation. With this method your daily benefit will increase 5% of the previous year's daily benefit amount. The premium will remain level.

The chart below summarizes the differences between no inflation, the 5% simple inflation method, and the 5% compound inflation method.

Assume a $100-per-day daily benefit amount.

Year	No inflation	5% Simple	5% Compound
1	$100.00	$105.00	$105.00
2	$100.00	$110.00	$110.25
3	$100.00	$115.00	$115.76
4	$100.00	$120.00	$121.55
5	$100.00	$125.00	$127.63
10	$100.00	$150.00	$162.89
15	$100.00	$175.00	$207.89
20	$100.00	$200.00	$265.33

Richard Nathanson

Recommendation... *If you are under 70 years old, you are exposed to inflationary risks. Because costs go up on a compounded basis, the only inflation option that makes sense is the compound inflation option. If you are over 70, and if you start out with an adequate daily benefit amount relative to costs, you might consider the no inflation option.*

Rating...Varies, depending on your age.

What Is Waiver of Premium?

Waiver of premium is the concept that once you are eligible for your benefit, you no longer have to pay your premium. However, there are a lot of variables and variations with respect to waiver of premium.

When Does the Waiver of Premium Start?

There are two ways of calculating when the waiver of premium can start.

The first is a certain number of days after you are <u>eligible for benefits</u>. This means that on the day your doctor certifies you are eligible for benefits, the number of days starts counting.

The second method is a certain number of days after you have <u>been receiving benefits</u>.

To illustrate the difference, let's assume that the number of days in the waiver of premium is 90 days. Let's also assume that you have a 90-day elimination period. Let's make two additional assumptions.

- First, you purchased the policy on January 1 and you had a stroke on March 1; thus you were eligible for benefits on March 1.

- Second, on June 1 the policy will start paying benefits because you satisfied the 90-day elimination period.

If your policy states that the waiver of premium will commence 90 days after you are eligible for benefits, you no longer have to pay the premium starting June 1.

If your policy states that the waiver of premium will commence 90 days after the benefits are paid, you no longer have to pay the premium starting September 1.

Recommendation... *It is slightly more valuable to have the waiver of premium start upon eligibility. The true difference, however, is that you would have to pay the premium 90 days longer if the waiver commences when the benefit is paid.*

Rating... 5

Is the Premium Waived Regardless of Where You Receive Care?

One would think that if you are receiving care, your premium would be waived no matter what location you chose to receive your care.

Unfortunately, that is not the case.

Every policy waives the premium if you are receiving your care in a nursing home. However, a number of companies do not waive the premium if you are receiving care in your home. In this case the policy would pay out the daily benefit amount, but you would also have to pay the premium.

Since home care is generally the location of preference, this could result in a major monetary difference among policies.

Richard Nathanson

Recommendation... *Make sure the premium is waived regardless of where you are receiving care.*

Rating...1

Is There Special Treatment for Married Couples?

With most policies, if one spouse requires care, then that spouse's premium is waived. The healthy spouse would continue to pay the premium.

Some policies go one step further for married couples. If one spouse needs care, the premium is waived for both spouses.

Recommendation... *If you are married, select a policy that waives the premium for both spouses when only one spouse needs care.*

Rating...1

What Is Restoration of Benefits?

In every policy you must select a duration of how long the policy will pay the daily benefit amount. The duration can range from as short as 1 year to as long as lifetime. If you select a duration of less than lifetime, a restoration of benefits feature is virtually essential.

Restoration of benefits works this way.

Let's assume you purchased a policy in 1997 with a 4-year duration. Ten years later you had a stroke, which required either home care or nursing home care. After satisfying the elimination period, the policy paid out for 1 year, after which time you recovered sufficiently that you didn't need any care. How many years' duration are left for the next time you get sick?

Can You Afford to Grow Old?

If you have restoration of benefits the answer is 4 years. If you don't have restoration of benefits, you have 3 years left.

Real-Life Story... *I meet with the Enids a couple of years ago. They requested that I see them to review their existing long term care policy. In the course of the meeting, Mrs. Enid told me that her husband had three strokes over the last 5 years and the policy had paid out a total of 3 years' worth of benefits. After each stroke, Mr. Enid recovered sufficiently that he no longer needed care. Mrs. Enid's concern was that, since they used 3 of their 4 years, what would happen if Mr. Enid needed care again?*

After reviewing her policy, I showed her that the policy had a restoration of benefits feature. Since Mr. Enid had recovered for a minimum of 6 months between episodes of needing care, all of the duration was restored. They were back to the original 4-year duration.

The following chart summarizes restoration of benefits.

Healthy

Sick

Satisfy Elimination Period

Policy Pays 1 Year

Healthy Again

1 Year Restored

If a company offers restoration of benefits, it could either be included in the base policy or a rider at an additional premium. There is also no limitation on how many times the policy can be restored.

To actually get the years restored, the process is the reverse of becoming eligible. You go to your doctor and the doctor must indicate that you no longer need assistance with the ADLs, you no longer have a cognitive impairment problem, or you no longer have a medical problem.

My experience with my clients has shown me that acute medical problems can happen very frequently, requiring short-term periods of care. Use of medical technology, particularly in the joint replacement area, is typical of people who need care and then recover. For these people, restoration of benefits is essential.

One last twist on restoration of benefits.

Real-Life Story... *I was having lunch a couple of months ago with a number of friends who are also in the business of selling long term care insurance. We started talking about the relative strength of various policies and got around to the restoration of benefits feature. Two of my friends like a particular company, and I asked them to describe how that company words the restoration of benefits. They went on to describe a typical scenario similar to the discussion in this chapter. I said to them, "Did you know that this company does not restore benefits during home care or assisted living care? They only restore the time used in a nursing home."*

Can You Afford to Grow Old?

These two agents were surprised that they didn't know this little quirk in the policy.

Note... The restoration of benefits feature is not always the same.

Recommendation... *If you pick a duration of less than lifetime, buy a policy that has restoration of benefits and restores it regardless of where you receive your care.*

Rating...1

How Is the Elimination Period Calculated?

The elimination period is the number of days that you must pay for your care before the policy pays. In many ways it is similar to a deductible.

Most people assume that this is a pretty straightforward area: of course policy A with a 100-day elimination period and policy B with a 100-day elimination period must be identical.

Right? Unfortunately, no.

Real-Life Story... *I met with Dr. Meisner a number of years ago to help him with filing a claim on a policy that was sold to him by another agent. In preparing the paperwork, he told me that 3 years ago he also filed a claim for care because of a broken hip. Everything went perfectly with that claim. The company paid out* *the daily benefit amount on the 101st day after satisfying the 100-day elimination period.*

Now Dr. Meisner needs care again because of knee replacement surgery. But fortunately, Dr. Meisner will probably need care for only 60 days as compared to the more extensive care following the hip replacement. Unfortunately I had to tell Dr. Meisner that his policy would not pay for his care following the knee replacement.

Needless to say, he wasn't very happy. His out-of-pocket expenses for those 60 days of care was going to be approximately $6,000.

How could this have happened?

All policies with a 100-day elimination period are not created equal. Policy (A) would work this way. "We have a 100-day elimination period and you must pay this amount every time you get sick. There is no limitation on how many times you would have to pay the 100-day elimination period." Policy (B) would work this way. "We have a 100-day elimination period but you only have to satisfy this amount once in your lifetime."

Dr. Meisner had policy (A).

The chart on the following page illustrates the possible differences in the two types of policies.

Can You Afford to Grow Old?

100-Day Elimination Period

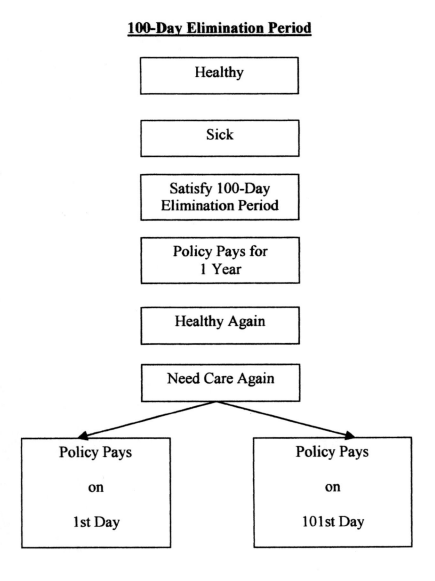

Healthy

Sick

Satisfy 100-Day
Elimination Period

Policy Pays for
1 Year

Healthy Again

Need Care Again

Policy Pays

on

1st Day

Policy Pays

on

101st Day

Recommendation... *If you select a policy that has an elimination period (1st-day coverage is available with most companies), make sure you have to pay that only once in your lifetime.*

Rating...1

Is There a Survivorship Feature?

This feature pertains only to married couples.

This is how most long term care policies work. Husband and wife both apply for long term care and are approved. Each spouse is issued a policy. Each spouse pays the premium. At some point, one spouse passes away. Obviously, no further payments are paid for the deceased spouse. The surviving spouse continues to pay for his/her long term care policy.

Some long term care policies go one step further.

Husband and wife both apply for long term care and are approved. Each spouse is issued a policy. Each spouse pays the premium. One spouse passes away. No further payments are paid for the deceased spouse. The surviving spouse's policy is fully paid up; **no further payments have to be made**.

Real-Life Story... *Mr. and Mrs. Daly were considering a purchase of long term care insurance. Mr. Daly was 71 years old. Mrs. Daly was 56 years old. When I told the Dalys that some policies have a survivorship feature, they knew they wanted a policy that had that feature. They were aware of certain realities. Men generally predecease women by 7 years. The 7 years, coupled with their 15-year difference in age, meant that for*

*possibly 22 years Mrs. Daly would not have to pay any premium
on her long term care policy.*

Recommendation... *If you are married, strongly consider a
policy with a survivorship feature.*

Rating...1

Are Homemaker Services Covered?

As discussed earlier in this chapter, you become eligible for your
benefits when you are unable to perform certain activities of
daily living. Eating, for example, is one of the activities that is
covered by every policy.

When I conduct seminars, I ask the audience if someone would
like to try to define eating. No one yet has answered it correctly.

Eating is defined succinctly as your ability to cut your food and
ingest it once it has been presented in front of you.

What is missing?

How did the food get in front of you? Obviously, someone
cooked the food. Cooking falls into a category called homemaker
services. If your policy does not contain homemaker services, the
daily benefit amount cannot be spent for homemaker services.

Homemaker services are, typically, shopping, cooking, cleaning,
doing the laundry, helping with correspondence, and helping
with managing money.

The importance of homemaker services is probably self-evident.
At the point when you need help with bathing, dressing, or
eating, you are going to need help with the homemaker services.

Richard Nathanson

A further issue is who can provide the homemaker services for you. In most policies, a licensed home health aid must help you with the homemaker services. However, some policies give you added flexibility in allowing friends, family members, or members of a religious organization to perform homemaker services. This added flexibility is attractive in two areas.

First, it would be a little nicer if friends or relatives could provide the shopping, cooking, cleaning, etc., and be compensated for it.

Second, and probably more important, this flexibility gives you more value from your policy. If a licensed home health aide must do the homemaker services for you, then he/she will probably charge $15 per hour. If the next-door neighbor can perform these services, then he/she may charge only $5 per hour. This way your daily benefit amount could last longer.

If a company offers homemaker services, it would either be included in the base policy for no additional premium, or the homemaker services would be a rider that must be purchased at an additional premium.

Recommendation... *Homemaker services are an integral part of care needs and must be part of the policy.*

Rating...1

What Is a Bed Reservation Benefit?

How does a bed reservation benefit work?

You are confined to a nursing home and you develop pneumonia and need to go to the hospital. A bed reservation benefit continues to pay your nursing home bed so that when you recover and are discharged from the hospital, you can return to the same nursing home.

Real-Life Story... *Mrs. Hart is the mother of a friend of mine and has been in a nursing home for 4 years. I remember vividly how difficult it was for the kids to make the decision that nursing home confinement was necessary. It was traumatic for the kids and heart-wrenching for the mother. But, like most nursing home residents, she adjusted within 1 week to her new environment.*

After being in the nursing home for 4 years, Mrs. Hart had a kidney problem and had to be hospitalized. She stayed in the hospital for 2 weeks. The day before her discharge, the kids called the nursing home just to tell them Mrs. Hart was ready to return.

Unfortunately the nursing home, which had a waiting list, had given Mrs. Hart's bed to another resident. The kids found another nursing home for Mrs. Hart, but it was agonizing for Mrs. Hart to go through the adjustment process again. She would never again be able to see the friends she had made during the last 4 years.

A bed reservation benefit assures that this does not happen.

Policies with this feature continue to pay your nursing home bed while you are in the hospital. They pay for a certain number of days per year, ranging from a low of 10 days per year to a high of 30 days per year.

Additionally, the number of days that are used can be calculated somewhat differently. Some policies deduct the number of days that are paid out to reserve your bed from the total number of days that you purchased. Other policies pay the bed reservation days in addition to the number of days you selected in your plan.

Recommendation... *Select the policy with the highest number of days for bed reservation. Ideally, the policy adds those days to the overall duration.*

Rating...4

Geographically Where Can You Receive Your Care?

Real-Life Story... *I met with Mr. Raye last year to review his long term care policy. He had a policy from an excellent company, the benefit levels were good, it had excellent contract features, and the price was good. So everything was perfect, right?*

Wrong! During the course of our discussion, Mr. Raye told me about his beautiful waterfront condominium in Mexico, where he spends 3 months a year, and he plans to permanently retire in Mexico. I asked Mr. Raye whether, if he needs care, he plans to come back to the United States.

His answer was no.

Now comes the problem.

I opened his policy to page 14 and the exclusion section of the policy. Unfortunately too many agents skip this section during the sales process. But it is in fact one of the more important sections because it describes when the policy will not pay.

Exclusion number 5 stated, "You cannot receive care outside the United States."

Can You Afford to Grow Old?

Although Mr. Raye had a good policy, it was the wrong one for him. He would be unable to receive his care where he intended to live: in Mexico.

All policies allow you to receive your care anywhere in the United States. If you buy the policy in Washington, you can move to Arizona and receive your care there. Some policies allow you to receive your care in Canada or the Territories of the United States. A small percentage of policies allow you to receive your care anywhere in the world.

Recommendation... *If you think there is a possibility that you may reside outside of the United States, it is critical to review where you can receive your care. Even if you have no plans to reside outside the United States, a policy that contains no geographic limitations would be of value if you travel outside the United States and you needed immediate care.*

Rating... 3

What Is Care Coordination?

Most companies promote a care coordination program. It is often discussed in their brochures and described as a benefit for you.

In many cases it only benefits the insurance company!

The company starts by describing the care coordination benefit as follows:

> "A case coordinator is a highly trained health care professional, pre-approved by us, whose main function is to work with you, your family, and your doctor in planning and arranging for

the individualized care you need. Your case
coordinator is experienced in selecting and hiring
care providers suited to your particular situation.
Help is provided in not only lining up the right
care at the outset, but also following your
progress and consulting with your doctor
as your needs change."

Sounds great, doesn't it? The only problem is, it goes on to say
that if you don't use this service, then the policy will pay 80% of
your daily benefit amount for care in your own home. If you use
the care coordinator, the company will pay 100% of the daily
benefit amount for home care.

Can you imagine that? You buy a policy for $100 per day and
unless you use their care coordination benefit, then they will pay
you only $80 per day for home care.

Other companies describe the care coordination process and
goals very similarly, but it is strictly a free-of-charge service and
you get all of your policy benefits whether you use care
coordination or not.

Real-Life Story... *I was assisting Mr. and Mrs. Brech in
processing a claim (I did not sell them the policy). As part of the
care coordination benefit, an individual from the insurance
company visited to assess a suitable home care plan. The care
coordinator assigned to the Brechs determined that 4 hours a
day of care was needed. The Brechs disagreed because they felt
they wanted 8 hours of care. They just were not comfortable
being left alone during the daytime (their daughter stayed with
them at night). Their policy stated that if you do not agree with
the plan of care as determined by the care coordinator, then they
will pay out the home care benefit at 80% of the amount
originally selected. Unfortunately, the Brechs received 20% less
benefit than what they thought they were entitled to.*

Can you Afford to Grow Old?

Recommendation... *Be leery of a policy that gives you everything that you think you are entitled to but only if you use care coordination.*

Rating... 2

What Is Guaranteed Renewable?

People buy long term care insurance to protect themselves against future events. Many companies underwrite the insurance so that policies are issued to people who probably will not need long term care for many years to come.

In return, the insured are expected to pay those premiums for many years, and when care is ultimately needed, they assume that the policy will pay benefits. They don't want to be in the position that, for reasons other than nonpayment of the premium, the insurance company cancels the contract.

A guaranteed renewable feature assures that the policy will be available when you need it.

As long as the policyholder pays the premium within the time frame stipulated in the contract, the insurer cannot cancel the contract.

This feature affords the consumer a great deal of protection.

Recommendation... *In the state of Washington, all policies are issued as guaranteed renewable.*

Richard Nathanson

What Is Nonforfeiture Protection?

Nonforfeiture protection refers to residual benefits that become available to policyholders if they stop paying premiums.

Although there are various types of nonforfeiture benefits, the most common is reduced paid-up protection.

In policies with a reduced paid-up feature, the policyholder is entitled to receive reduced levels of benefits if the policyholder discontinues making premium payments. For example, a policy may give you a 3% per year reduced paid-up benefit. Therefore, if you pay the premium for 10 years and originally purchased $100 per day, then after 10 years your reduced paid-up benefit is $30 per day.

Does this help you out in any meaningful way? I don't think so.

People buy long term care insurance to protect assets. If $100 per day covers the risk, would $30 per day do any good in protecting your assets?

I don't think it would do much good at all.

With a $30 per day benefit, you would be looking at $70 per day out-of-pocket expense or $25,550 per year. A 4-year stay in a nursing home would still cost you $102,200 out of your pocket.

So much for protecting your assets!

Recommendation... *Don't buy long term care insurance unless it is affordable and you can continue to expect to make the premium payments. A reduced paid-up option will provide no* *meaningful protection against the cost of needing long term care, and it adds a significant cost to the premium.*

Rating... 9

What Are Other Available Benefits?

Companies offer a variety of other benefits that, in the aggregate, do not add a lot of value to a policy. However, I will briefly highlight some of them.

Caregiver Training... Pays a certain amount, generally a multiple of a home care daily benefit amount, when a family member needs training to provide care in lieu of nursing home care or home health care.

Emergency Response System... Pays for the rental of an emergency response system, like a medic call button, when you are receiving home care. Generally, the amount is limited to $25 per month.

Ambulance Service... Pays actual charges for ambulance service to and from a nursing home. Generally, it is limited to $250 per trip for up to 4 trips per calendar year.

Equipment... Pays for the purchase or rental of supportive equipment to allow you to stay at home. Generally, it pays a set amount for life, based on a multiple of your daily benefit amount.

Annual Wellness Benefit... Pays for a routine physical to help keep you in good health. Generally, it is a set dollar amount available per year.

Prescription Drug Benefit... Pays for prescription drugs while you are receiving home care. Generally pays a fixed monthly dollar amount.

Recommendation... *If the policy has any of these additional benefits, that's great. But don't buy a policy just because of these features.*

Rating...10

Chapter 10

Tax-Qualified Plans vs. Non-Qualified Plans

On August 21, 1996, President Clinton signed the Health Insurance Portability and Accountability Act of 1996, or HR3103, better known as the Kassebaum-Kennedy legislation. The act sets forth guidelines for "Qualified Long Term Care Policies."

The federal government recognized that long term health care is a major problem. It also rightfully concluded that with the demise of Mrs. Clinton's attempt at health care reform, a national subsidized program for long term care was not going to happen. Consequently, in an effort to encourage consumers to be proactive in dealing with long term care needs, certain "tax incentives" were incorporated into HR3103, designed to encourage the purchase of long term care insurance.

Although the intent was good, like many pieces of legislation, the language in the bill is flawed. In reality, it could adversely affect your ability to collect your benefit if you purchase a "Qualified Long Term Care Policy."

First, here are the positive features of a "Qualified Long Term Care Policy."

If you purchase a "qualified" plan, then a portion of the premium may be income-tax-deductible. The tax-deductible portion of the premium would be added to the combined total of unreimbursed medical and dental expenses. If this amount exceeds 7.5% of adjusted gross income, then this amount is deductible as an itemized deduction on Schedule A on your IRS form 1040. The amount of the long term care premium that is includable in the unreimbursed medical and dental expenses is limited as follows:

Age	Premium Limit
40 and below	$ 200
41-50	$ 375
51-60	$ 750
61-70	$2,000
71 and over	$2,500

These are the 1997 limits, which are indexed to inflation.

The biggest problem with the deductibility of the premium is that most people who purchase long term care insurance do not itemize their deductions on Schedule A. Generally, unless you have excessive medical and dental bills or have substantial interest expense (a mortgage on your home), then the allowed standard deduction probably exceeds the itemized deduction amount.

<u>In general, the deductibility of the premium is not an advantage.</u>

The second "advantage" of qualified plans is that if the policy pays out benefits (you are eligible and the policy is paying the daily benefit amount), then the benefits are income-tax-free. The legislation is presently silent as to how benefits on non-qualified plans will be taxed. Most tax experts with whom I have consulted have concluded that if the benefits are includable as taxable income, then the expense of the care would be tax-deductible as a medical expense on Schedule A.

Can You Afford to Grow Old?

Unfortunately, this is one of the gray areas that will have to be addressed later by Congress. Despite the potential tax advantages, for the reasons discussed below, the disadvantage of restricting your ability to have a claim paid under a "qualified" plan completely outweighs, in my opinion, any tax advantage in a "qualified" plan.

First, a Word of Caution

Some insurance companies issue only "qualified" plans, some insurance companies issue only "non-qualified" plans, while some insurance companies issue both. The problem is that if an agent can sell you only a "qualified" plan he or she will push that plan even though it may be against your best interests.

Why do I say this...?

The eligibility triggers are different between "qualified" and "non-qualified" plans.

Qualified Plans	vs.	Non-Qualified Plans
ADL trigger requires substantial assistance.		ADL trigger requires any amount of assistance.
Cognitive impairment trigger requires a severe cognitive impairment.		Cognitive impairment trigger requires any amount of a cognitive impairment.
Medical necessity benefit trigger is not available.		Medical necessity benefit trigger is available.
Functional loss must last at least 90 days.		Functional loss can last less than 90 days.

Richard Nathanson

The "qualified" plans include more severe eligibility language, which unfortunately is not defined in the statute.

What is substantial assistance as compared to any amount of assistance?

What is severe cognitive impairment as compared to any amount of cognitive impairment?

Think back to some of my real-life stories...

Real-Life Story... *My aunt who passed away from ovarian cancer had a medical problem but did not have an ADL dependency or a cognitive impairment problem. With a "qualified" plan my aunt would not have received any benefits because the medical necessity benefit trigger is not available.*

Real-Life Story... *Mr. Evans' cognitive impairment wasn't severe enough for the insurance company's doctor to determine it. With a "qualified" plan Mr. Evans would not have received any benefits, as his cognitive impairment was not severe.*

Real-Life Story... *Dr. Meisner's knee replacement surgery will require care for only 60 days, not the 90 days required under HR3103. With a "qualified" plan Dr. Meisner would not receive any benefits.*

To emphasize the importance of greater ease of eligibility in a non-qualified plan, I quote a leading long term care company that includes medical necessity as a benefit trigger: "Forty % of our claims for home care and 20% of our claims for nursing home care would not have been paid under one of the qualified plans."

Can You Afford to Grow Old?

Being denied a benefit between 20% and 40% of the time if you purchased a qualified plan is an incredible deterrent to selecting a qualified plan.

Recommendation... *Buy the best non-qualified plan available.*

Rating...1

Richard Nathanson

Caveat Emptor...Let the Buyer Beware

The purpose of this book is to educate people on the topic of long term care. Education is the key, because although I would like to think that every sales representative is looking out for the best interest of the client, unfortunately that is not always the case.

The following section includes some of the gray areas in which agents sometimes cross the line.

How Does Alternate Plan of Care Work?

Alternate plan of care is in virtually every policy. Detailed below is an actual definition from one of the leading long term care companies.

> "If you would otherwise qualify for benefits, we will consider paying for cost of services you require under a written alternative plan of care.... Alternative care may include but not be limited to (1) special treatments, (2) different sites of care, or (3) modifications to your residence to accommodate your needs."

Real-Life Story... *Mr. White lived in a beautiful two-story home that was built around the turn of the century. However, he was concerned about the increasing difficulty he was having in* *climbing the stairs. Eventually the problem was getting to the point where he might have to seek care in some type of facility. He called me up and we filed a claim under the alternate plan of care provision. We asked that a chair lift be installed and that the bathrooms be modified to ultimately accommodate a walker and wheelchair. We also asked that handrails be installed. The company paid for this under the alternate plan of care.*

This is the appropriate use of the alternate plan of care rider. If the company did not make the renovations, Mr. White would have ended up in a nursing care facility. The company would have paid out $4,000 per month for his care. Instead, it made the renovations at the cost of $3,750. The insurance company made an economic decision that it was in its best interest to spend $3,750 once for renovations rather than spend $4,000 per month for Mr. White's care.

Real-Life Story... *I was referred to Mrs. Holmes, who was considering a purchase of long term care insurance. She had previously met with another agent, who put together a plan for her that she thought sounded very reasonable. She wanted a plan that would allow her to receive her care wherever she needed, but particularly wanted home care. This particular company structures policies in such a way that you purchase the nursing home care portion and if you want home care you purchase the home care rider. <u>The home health care rider requires an additional premium that Mrs. Holmes did not purchase</u>. The agent reassured Mrs. Holmes that she could receive her care in her home. He pointed to the alternate plan of care: "alternative care may include (2) different sites of care." He said. "This is how the home care works...the different sites would be your home."*

I asked Mrs. Holmes one question. "Does it make sense that you can receive home care under your policy and not have to

Can You Afford to Grow Old?

purchase the home care rider that the company charges 50% extra for?"

Alternative plan of care would not cover home care in this situation. No insurance company is going to give you a home care benefit that you didn't pay extra for unless, in some fashion, it will save them money.

Recommendation... *Don't rely on alternate plan of care for anything more than what it is.*

Rating... 1

Are You Comparing Apples to Apples?

Some agents find themselves in a competitive situation and try to make the sale based only on cost. The lowest price makes the sale. You need to make sure you are comparing apples to apples.

Which of these two policies, based on cost, would you buy?

Policy A	Policy B
Age 69	Age 69
$100 daily benefit	$100 daily benefit
4 years	4 years
100-day elimination	100-day elimination
5% inflation	5% inflation
Cost $2,250	**Cost $1,980**

Looks simple: everything is the same, pick Policy B at $1,980.

Real-Life Story... *I met Mrs. Bruce a couple of times and she ended up purchasing a policy. Halfway through the underwriting, she called me and said she just received a quote over the phone for "exactly" the same benefits that I showed her but it was at a substantially lower price. I went back to see her. Yes, the daily benefit was the same; yes, the duration was the same; yes, the elimination period was the same; and Mrs. Bruce had asked for a price that included 5% inflation. The only problem was the agent on the phone quoted 5% simple inflation and I quoted 5% compound inflation. All of a sudden we were not comparing apples to apples.*

As it turns out, Policy A and Policy B are both from the same company and the exact same policy form. The only difference is that Policy A includes 5% compound inflation and Policy B includes 5% simple inflation.

Recommendation... *Make sure you compare apples to apples.*

Rating...1

Will Your Premiums Stay Level?

Real-Life Story... *I met with Mrs. Austin to discuss long term care. Her husband was not insurable because of multiple strokes and confinement in a wheelchair. A prior agent was recommending a good policy and was pushing to take the application by saying, "You need to buy now, we can lock in your age and the premiums will never go up." I asked Mrs. Austin to show me where in the disclosure form or the product brochure it said that the premiums would never go up. She couldn't, because they can go up.*

Can You Afford to Grow Old?

Premiums can go up and, in fact, with some companies they have gone up. Don't let an agent tell you something to the contrary.

The bottom line is that besides picking the policy and picking the benefit levels, **you must also pick the agent**.

Richard Nathanson

Chapter 12

Distribution Sources for Purchasing Long Term Care Insurance

There are three ways you can purchase long term care insurance.

Direct Mail

As the name implies, you receive the sales material in the mail. You read the product description, select benefit levels, calculate the premium, and mail the application to the company.

The problem with direct mail is that long term care is a complicated area. Hopefully the preceding pages in this book have given you an idea of the differences that are available in different products. Unless you make yourself an expert on long term care, it will be very difficult to discern the subtle differences between policies.

Captive Sales Agent

A captive sales agent represents one company. That agent will present to you the features and benefits of only one plan. If his policy does not have a certain positive feature, i.e., the survivorship feature or restoration of benefits, he or she will not mention that competitors have it.

This puts the responsibility of product comparison on you.

Broker

The advantage of using an agent who has access to virtually all the available long term care companies is that the consumer is in the position to truly compare the various policies based on cost and features.

The broker truly does not have an agenda as to which policy to sell. Commissions are essentially similar, which alleviates a bias on the part of the sales agent. Further, an agent who has access to almost all of the companies probably specializes in long term care. This gives the consumer access to all the latest trends in an area of insurance that is changing very rapidly.

Recommendation...*Use a broker with whom you are comfortable. Do not hesitate to assess his or her credentials and references.*

Rating...1

Financial Strength of the Company

The financial strength of a company is very important.

Financial strength goes to the heart of why you purchase a policy. You want the company to honor your claim in the event that you need care.

The financial health of an insurance company can be measured in a number of ways.

• AM Best rating...This is an insurance rating service that measures financial strength. Its ratings represent the current and independent opinion of an insurance company's financial strength and ability to meet obligations to policyholders.

Recommendation... *Select a policy that is rated at least Excellent by AM Best.*

• Claims paying... Some companies publish statistics that measure the overall percentage of claims paid.

Recommendation... *Select a company that publishes its claim paying record, and make sure it is at least 90% of all claims submitted.*

• Complaint records...The insurance commission's office maintains a record of the number of complaints filed against a particular company. Review that information to get a sense of customer satisfaction with the company.

Recommendation... *Select a company that has a low number of consumer complaints.*

Rating... 1

Chapter 14

The Application Process

You have gone through the hardest part.

You analyzed the risks of needing long term care and have determined that, for peace of mind and to protect your assets, the purchase of long term care insurance is appropriate.

You reviewed in detail the features and benefits of the various policies and have selected the one that best fits your needs.

What's next?

You must submit an application. Contrary to property and casualty insurance, no long term care agent has the authority to "bind" the insurance company. The application is the procedure that allows the insurance company to determine if it is willing to insure you.

The application consists of a number of different and important sections.

The first part consists of general biographical information like name, address, social security number, height, weight, etc.

The second part is the medical section. You must disclose medical conditions that you have been treated for. This section is critical to both the insurance company and you. Always fully disclose all medical conditions. If in any doubt, disclose it. The failure to properly disclose your medical history could invalidate a claim. The insurance company uses the medical section to underwrite your application.

The third section is a description of the medications that you are taking. The medications tend to correlate with the medical conditions that are listed.

With the application, all companies require a deposit. In all cases the deposit is 100% refundable. If, after you submit the application, you hit the lottery and don't need long term care insurance, you can get all your money back. If the company declines your application, you get back 100% of your deposit.

In fact, even after you receive your policy and have fully paid for it, you have an additional 30 days to change your mind and receive a 100% refund. Bear in mind the 30 days starts from when you receive your policy and sign the delivery receipt, not the day the policy was approved.

The next step is for the agent to submit the application to the company.

The next part of the process can vary, depending upon the company, but generally consists of the following steps.

Telephone Interview... *The company contacts the applicant and verifies the information on the application. They ask you more in-depth questions than were asked on the application.*

Personal Interview... *Depending on your medical conditions, age, and answers to the telephone questions, a face-to-face interview may be required. Generally, if you are 75 years of age or older, the personal interview will include some cognitive/memory testing.*

Can You Afford to Grow Old?

Attending Physician's Statement (APS)... *This is the request for medical records. The company requests from your primary physician copies of your medical records. From the medical records the company is able to assess your overall health.*

The entire process takes between 4 and 6 weeks, although I have seen it take up to 8 weeks on some occasions.

Once you are approved, the agent will contact you and review the actual policy. Make sure you see in the policy the features that made you determine that the policy was the right one for you.

Richard Nathanson

Chapter 15

Underwriting

Underwriting is the process by which the insurance company evaluates the applicant's health history and determines whether it can extend coverage.

Surprisingly, there are great differences among the various companies in acceptable medical conditions.

For example, strokes--whether it is a TIA or a CVA--represent a common medical condition that affects senior citizens. Five of the leading long term care companies rate the medical acceptability of this condition as follows:

- Insurable immediately if no residuals
- Insurable if longer than 12 months ago and no residuals
- Insurable if longer than 18 months ago and no residuals
- Insurable if longer than 24 months ago and no residuals
- Not insurable at all

This points out that it is very important to review all of your options even if you have been turned down before for long term care insurance. My experience is that more than 90% of applicants can get covered for long term care.

Included in the appendix of this book is a condensed underwriting guide from one of the leading long term care companies.

Recommendation... *If you have any medical concerns, fully disclose your health history to your agent so that he or she can find the company that most likely will insure you.*

Rating...1

Richard Nathanson

Chapter 16

Epilogue

Throughout this book I have tried to identify why long term care is such a problem. It is a fact that needing long term care can be a financial time bomb. The probability of needing care is very high and the cost of care is very high.

I have a unique passion for the importance of long term care. In the prologue to this book I discussed the situation of my wife's grandmother. Our family spent $216,000 for her care. Our family did not have long term care insurance.

My hope is that this book educated you on the problem of long term care and the solution for dealing with it. It is my profound hope that you or your family never has to pay the financial consequences of not having long term care insurance.

Richard Nathanson

Glossary of Terms

"Activities of daily living" (ADL)-- Measure of a person's level of independence/dependence. Includes individual tasks such as bathing, transferring, dressing, toileting, eating, and maintaining continence.

"Acute care"-- Care provided for patients who are not medically stable. These patients require frequent monitoring by health care professionals in order to maintain their health status.

"Adult day care"-- Daytime, community-based program for functionally impaired adults that provides a variety of health, nutrition, social, and related services in a protective setting to those who are otherwise being cared for by family members. Its purpose is to enable individuals to remain at home and in the community and to encourage family members to care for them by providing relief from the burden of constant care.

"Assisted living" -- Residential care settings providing personal care services, shopping, housekeeping, and transportation. Assisted living also may be called board and care, personal care, or residential health care.

"Benefit maximum"-- Amount of money or days of care beyond which an insurance policy will not pay benefits.

"Benefit trigger"-- Point at which criteria used to determine eligibility for benefits is met.

"Care advisement services"-- includes, but is not limited to, a comprehensive individualized face-to-face assessment conducted in the insured's place of residence, which takes an all-inclusive look at the patient's total needs and resources, and links the patient to a full range of appropriate services using all available funding sources. The assessment is evaluated at least once every 6 months. When desired by the insured and when it is determined to be necessary by the care adviser, care advisement services include coordination of appropriate services and ongoing monitoring of the delivery of such services.

"Care advisor" or "case coordinator" -- An individual qualified by training and/or experience to coordinate the overall medical, personal, and social service needs of the long term care patient. Such coordination activities include but are not limited to: assessing the individual's condition to determine what services and resources are necessary and by whom they might most appropriately be delivered; coordination of elements of a treatment or care plan and referral to the appropriate medical or social services personnel or agency; control coordination of patient services and continued monitoring of the patient to assess progress and assure that services are delivered. Such activities are conducted in consultation with the attending physician.

"Chronic care" or "maintenance care"-- Care that is necessary to support an existing level of health and is intended to preserve that level from further failure or decline. The care provided is usually for a long-drawn-out or lingering disease or infirmity showing little change or slowly progressing with little likelihood of complete recovery, whether such care is provided in an institution or is community-based and whether such care is skilled or custodial/personal.

"Cognitive impairment"-- Problems with attention that affect memory or other loss of intellectual capacity, which requires supervision to help or protect the impaired person.

Can You Afford to Grow Old?

"Community-based care"-- Services including but not limited to: (a) home delivered nursing services or therapy; (b) custodial or personal care; (c) day care; (d) home and chore aid services; (e) nutritional services, both in-home and in a communal dining setting; (f) respite care; (g) adult day health care services; or (h) other similar services furnished in a homelike or residential setting that does not provide overnight care. Such services are provided at all levels of care, from skilled care to custodial or personal care.

"Continuum of care" -- Interrelated and connected range of services, from home and community-based programs to institutionalization, needed by older adults at various stages of disability.

"Convalescent care" -- Non-acute care that is prescribed by a physician and is received during the period of recovery from an illness or injury when improvement can be anticipated, whether such care is skilled or custodial/personal, and whether such care is provided in an institutional care facility or is community-based.

"Coordination of benefits" -- Method of integrating benefits payable under more that one health insurance source so that the insured's benefits from all sources do not exceed 100% of allowable expenses.

"Custodial care" or "personal care" -- Care that is mainly for the purpose of meeting daily living requirements. Persons without professional skills or training may provide this level of care. Examples are help in walking, getting out of bed, bathing, dressing, eating, meal preparation, toileting, and taking medications. Such care is intended to maintain and support an existing level of health or to preserve the patient from further decline. Custodial or personal care services are those that may be recommended by the care advisor in consultation with the patient's attending physician and are not primarily for the convenience of the insured or the insured's family.

"Elimination period" -- Waiting period or the initial number of days before benefits are paid by an insurance company once the insured becomes eligible for benefits.

"Guaranteed renewable" -- Renewal of a contract may not be declined by an insurer for any reason except for nonpayment of premium, but the insurer may revise rates on a claim basis.

"Home care services" or **"personal care services"** -- Services of a personal nature including, but not limited to, homemaker services, assistance with the activities of daily living, respite care services, or any other nonmedical services provided to ill, disabled, or infirm persons, which services enable those persons to remain in their own residences consistent with their desires, abilities, and safety. An insurer may require that services are provided by or under the direction of a home health care agency regulated by our state, or that services are administered in accordance with a plan of treatment developed by or with the assistance of health care professionals.

"Home health care" -- Includes but is not limited to, any of the following health or medical services: nursing services, home health aid services, physical therapy, occupational therapy, speech therapy, respiratory therapy, nutritional services, medical or social services, and medical supplies or equipment services. An insurer may require that services are provided by or under the direction of a regulated home health care agency regulated by the state, or that services are administered in accordance with a plan of treatment developed by or with the assistance of health care professionals.

Can You Afford to Grow Old?

"Inflation protection" -- Insurance provision that allows policyholders to increase insurance benefits over time to offset higher service costs associated with inflation.

"Institutional care" -- Care provided in a hospital, nursing home, or other facility certified or licensed by the state primarily affording diagnostic, preventive, therapeutic, rehabilitative, maintenance, or personal care services. Such a facility provides 24-hour nursing services on its premises or in facilities available to the institution on a formal prearranged basis.

"Instrumental activities of daily living (IADL)"-- Measure of a person's level of independence/dependence. Includes activities such as ability to do housework, prepare meals, manage money, and use the telephone.

"Means test" -- Measure of income and assets to determine eligibility for government benefit programs.

"Respite care" -- Short-term care required in order to maintain the health or safety of the patient and to give temporary relief to the primary caretaker from his or her care-taking duties.

"Skilled care" -- Care for an illness or injury that requires the training and skills of a licensed professional nurse, is prescribed by a physician, is medically necessary for the condition or illness of the patient, and is available on a 24-basis.

"Skilled nursing facility" -- Institutional but not inpatient hospital care, requiring limited medical attention that is provided under supervision of registered nursing personnel or a physician.

"Spend down" -- Depletion of assets to pay for long term care, after which a person becomes eligible for Medicaid.

"Upgrade" -- Formal process by which an insurer allows policyholders with an earlier generation of product to purchase a new policy, generally without meeting some of the requirements (e.g., no underwriting, maintaining the purchase price based on the original age).

Sample Underwriting Guide

Condition	Action
Acquired Immune Deficiency Syndrome	No
ADL Deficiencies	No
Adult Day Care	No
Alcoholism with recovery 3 years	Yes
Alzheimer's Disease	No
Amputation--Accidental	Yes
Amputation--Caused by Diabetes	No
Anemia	Maybe
Aneurysm	Maybe
Angina Pectoris	Yes
Angioplasty	Yes
Arrhythmia	Yes
Arteriosclerosis	Maybe
Arthritis	Yes
Asthma	Yes
Bursitis	Yes
Cancer	Maybe
Cataracts	Yes
Cerebral Palsy	No
Cerebral Vascular Disease	Maybe
Cirrhosis of the Liver	No
COPD	Maybe
Crohn's Disease	Maybe
Dementia (Senility)	No
Diabetes	Yes
Diverticulitis	Yes
Emphysema (mild)	Yes

Richard Nathanson

Condition	Action
Epilepsy	Yes
Gall Bladder Trouble or Gallstones	Yes
Glaucoma	Yes
Home Health Care	Maybe
Hepatitis A	Maybe
Herniated Disc, operated	Yes
High Blood Pressure, controlled	Yes
Hypoglycemia	Yes
Ileitis	Yes
Joint Replacement	Yes
Kidney Disorder, requiring dialysis	No
Kidney Stones	Yes
Leukemia	Maybe
Lymphoma	Maybe
Macular Degeneration	Maybe
Memory Loss	No
Migraine Headaches	Yes
Multiple Myeloma	No
Multiple Sclerosis	No
Muscular Dystrophy	No
Myasthenia Gravis	No
Nephritis	Maybe
Neuritis	Yes
Nursing Home Confinement	Maybe
Organ Transplant	No
Osteomyelitis, active	Yes
Osteoporosis	Maybe
Oxygen, use of	No
Pancreatitis, recovered	Yes
Paraplegia	No
Parkinson's Disease	No
Peripheral Vascular Disease	Yes
Phlebitis	Yes

Can You Afford to Grow Old?

Condition	Action
Polycythemia	Maybe
Prostate Disorders	Maybe
Quadriplegia	No
Retinal Detachment	Yes
Sciatica	Yes
Scleroderma	No
Senile Dementia	No
Stroke/CVA/TIA	Maybe
Thrombocytopenia	Maybe
Tuberculosis, recovered	Yes
Ulcers (gastric or duodenal)	Yes
Varicose Veins	Yes
Vertigo	Yes
Wheelchair	No

Richard Nathanson

About the Author

An Overview of My Practice

My practice revolves around the concept of needs-based financial planning. I help my clients identify their goals and objectives, preparing individualized concepts designed to accomplish them, and continually monitoring the plan through an ongoing relationship.

My clients most appreciate my services for the problems I solve rather than the products I sell.

My Education

- Bachelor of science in economics, Northeastern University

- Master's in business administration, Suffolk University

- College of Financial Planning, Boston University

- Stonier Graduate School of Banking, Rutgers University

- Graduate School of Banking, University of Oklahoma

Richard Nathanson

My Credentials

- Licensed Life and Health Agent

- NASD series 7 Securities License

- Licensed Real Estate Broker

- Certified Commercial Lender

My Job Experience

- Comptroller of the Currency, US Treasury Department

- Bank of Boston, Senior Executive, Commercial Banking

- Principal, The Abby Group

My Practical Experience

- Life Insurance Planning

- Long Term Care Insurance Planning

- Retirement and Estate Planning

- Debtor/Creditor Planning

- Commercial Lending and Loan Workout Planning

102

Can You Afford to Grow Old?

Order Form

To order additional copies of **Can You Afford to Grow Old?**
complete the information below. Please print.

Ship to:

Name   _____

Address   _____

City   _____

State   _____

Zip Code   _____

Phone Number _____

Please rush me _____ additional copies of
Can You Afford to Grow Old? @ $14.99 each $_____

Postage & Handling   @ $ 2.50 each $_____

WA state residents add 8.6% sales tax $_____

Total Amount Enclosed $_____

Make checks payable to: ***Richard M. Nathanson***

Mail Order Form To:

Richard M. Nathanson
24122 W. Graystone Lane
Woodway, WA 98020
~~(425)-672-9304~~
(206) 546-5004

Can You Afford to Grow Old?

Richard Nathanson

Free Consultation

I offer a free-of-charge consultation to customize an individual solution to the problem of long term care. Please complete the information below and mail it to the address shown.

Name _____

Address _____

City _____

State _____

Zip Code _____

Phone Number_____

Mail Free Consultation Form To:

Richard M. Nathanson
24122 W. Graystone Lane
Woodway, WA 98020
~~**(425)-672-9304**~~

(206) 546-5004